When the Cats Yawn

poems by

Kate McNairy

Finishing Line Press
Georgetown, Kentucky

When the Cats Yawn

ACKNOWLEDGMENTS

Thank you to the periodicals for publishing my poems included in this
collection:

Raven's Perch—"A Still Life"
Bluebird Word—"Autumn"
Scarlet Dragonfly—haiku "Across the moonlight…"

Publisher: Leah Huete de Maines
Editor: Christen Kincaid
Cover Art: Jon Sargalis
Author Photo: Jon Sargalis
Cover Design: Elizabeth Maines McCleavy

Order online: www.finishinglinepress.com
also available on amazon.com

Author inquiries and mail orders:
Finishing Line Press
PO Box 1626
Georgetown, Kentucky 40324
USA

Contents

"Sometimes it seems as if in her work a cat came out at us speaking English."
R.P. Blackmur upon reading Emily Dickinson

Awaken

Pouring coffee
into my blue & white
flecked mug

seems endless,

& with all I have
squandered
in my life,

there is still
as much as
necessary

to bear me through.

Keep On Going

I will not fall down.
I will not trip.

I will face my bullshit.

Here is, is here—
all of me

that I can put up with.

Brother and Sisters

We were built
in a wary home.

White pillars still
 buttress the doorway.

Now each kept secret
breathes far from.

Stand Tall

Look-see,
that delicious dress.

I tailored the fabric—
a few dozen frayed
swatches—

bright red clothing of defiance.

The Fixer

Two sparrows
fuss among
yellow & orange
leaves.

My shadow
draws a
red circle,

spots
a go-between,
in grasses.

The birds

stilled,
a standoff.

Feral Cats

At nightfall, after the feral cats have had their fill of pigeons—

                           they sit in the middling of
                                        birch branches
where the grass ends & the moon begins,
                               licking their paws bloodless.

A Study

I sketch
a few bumblebees
nesting,

so that when they
take wing

their absence
feels less.

Swim

Below moonlight a river moves,

fitful waters.

Amidst the hoo-ha
I toss about,

lost in the din of stars & waves.

Yet, I make it to my wordless room,
in the shallows of the riverbank—

lapping waters
  ease.

Boston 3:00 a.m.

She walks from her apartment
after a day of work—insomnia,
empty streets,
following the Charles.
Abruptly, she stops, turns,
strips. Her black turtleneck,
olive linen slacks, ivory
lace bra & panties,
tossed over a bridge—
free, free as a red winged blackbird,
her body belongs to the night.

A Poem
for Jon

I covet the love letter from my apple tree—
such juicy red fruit.

Closing my eyes, I wait…
seems an eternity to see you.

If I had you from the start,
I would have loved that—

now, my whole life quakes.

Silence

breathes in & out of me,
calls up the past, a darkened memory.

Listen to the echoes of your own dim past.
We'll nestle, sleep in each other's arms,

the pair of us forgives,
letting go.

A Candle

Whether it's day or dark, I keep a candle inside me,
a lasting, flickering light.

In the tumult of living, I struggle to listen to
the quiet,

my safe & sane

lighted candle.

A Still Life

a bowl of fruit
beside a dog.

Sit-stay, I say

but she escapes,
tears thru the yard
with an apple.

Fresh Laundry

After "Windy Day" by Charles Simic

Two sets of skivvies
one blue, one white

          dance in & out
          on the clothesline—

letting the neighbors
know.

Fruit

I carry a basket of fruit.
It topples over,
an abundance of
mangos, plantains, papaya.
You, a Samaritan,
bend down.
We gather it all up.
As we touch—the hair
on our hands tingles.

Autumn

brings a screen
door to lock up—

my shadow flees
an open window,

twists & turns
in breezes—

each fallen leaf
passes.

September Garden

Once an acre, now pared
back to three yards—

a tomato thrives—
we taste it,

feel our fleshy bodies,
the pulp, seeds—

we are eager,
naked & ready.

November Dusk

In a stand of wind-swept

                  shivering birch trees,

      all my naked branches,

         twist their light up & out.

Lit

This evening I swill

                            a glass of winter,

      twirl on its early

            dark & cold.

                           Stars scatter

      the blackness—

Loss

Uncanny how each snowflake
glistens, a singular
pattern, a code.

In this long-lasting disquiet
winter collapses,
folds.

Faith

In doubt

I gather

my arthritic dog

close to my chest.

The White Oak

A nuthatch touches
down on the tree,

a tree that shoulders
my secrets.

Below in the grass,
the green shoots
tell.

Havoc

All the nuances
of black holes, speed—
must drive the gods crazy.
Zip & unzip
the universe,
tear at its
uncertain seams.

Haiku

across the moonlight,
a bold comet skims colors—
lone howler monkey.

Haiku

listen—
a lake, smooth & clear,
each word drowns another.

Haiku

tuck in the night,
fold it over,
feel the dark full.

Hunger

Hair in dreadlocks, the
young fisherman in Belize
cleans snapper
on the dock at noon.
Black frigate birds cry,
their long, tilted wings
swoop forward, what's left.

My Ninety-Six-Year-Old Mother Plays Poker Online at Her Bedside Table

Gambling for nickels, she lets the cursor fly.
Her king of diamonds wins the latest hand.

Then, she flips open the wild card,
the dark queen of spades.

She slides the arrow from hearts to clubs,
praying for the jackpot as her world darkens.

High School Reunion

Once his brown mop of hair fell to his shoulders.

Fifty years later,
unrecognizable, hair gray & wiry.

Those eyes,

still deep endless cups of black coffee.

Education

Lisa signed
'never change, be you'
in my yearbook—

Yet remaining
the same got me
nowhere.

Silver-Haired

As an
irascible
birch tree—

I'm not ready
to go, yet—

my black & white
spindly branches

whip up
paper-thin leaves,
in disdain.

Cure-All

In night's deep uncertainty
I swallow five pills—green, blue,
copper, round & oval.

Come morning,
I guzzle three capsules
& two powdered drinks.

Yet—if I forget all the chemicals
I will kiss everyone
  Goodbye.

Kate McNairy lives in upstate New York, Ballston Spa where she shares a home with her life partner, Jon and the whimsical cat, Tigger.

Kate is a minimalist poet inspired by Emily Dickinson and William Carlos Williams among others and she has published the chapbooks: *June Bug* (2014), *Light to Light* (2016) and *My Wolf* (2021). Her poems have appeared in several journals including *Third Wednesday, Raven's Perch and Bluebird Word, Scarlet Dragonfly*, and *Local Gems* among others. As a freelance writer, Kate published articles in several newspapers including the *Albany Times Union*. She was a featured poet at Café Lena, Third Thursdays and Bright Hill Press Literary Center. Kate was on the editorial board of The Apple Tree. She has a B.A. and M.A. degrees from SUNY Albany.

In another life, Kate was an administrative assistant for AA White Sox, a minor league team.

A special thanks to Jon.